Fan Tales

Philippe Mesmer

Publishing director:
Jean-Paul Manzo

Text by: Philippe Mesmer

Designed by: Sébastien Ceste

Photographic credits

ISBN 1 85995 840 0

*I*n the 19th century, fans were to women what the sword was to men: an 'instrument of persuasion'. That at least is how the society of the day described an object that had become, in the hands of women, the 'armed hand' of seduction. However, there is a whole history to tell before we reach that point. In ancient times, the heavy, muggy heat of Egypt forced Pharaohs to take refuge in the gentle breeze created by a palm leaf held by a slave whose sole job was to take care of his divine master's well-being.

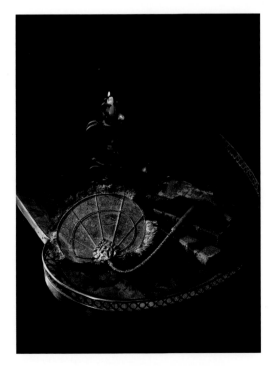

1. Fan in mica.
End of the 17th century -
beginning of the 18th century.
Chandelier and books.
Holland, 17th century.

2. Screen in mica representing figures of women. Holland (Colony of Indochina?),
End of the 17th — beginning of the 18th century.
Wood, mica, paper-muché, cardboard, leather, silk, painting, sculpture, gilding.
36.6 x 33 cm.
Acquired in 1968 by M. I. Kalinina. 9456/Pz-254

On the sheet of transparent mica, surrounded by a fringe of multicolored silk, two
figures   half-naked women and motifs of vegetation are drawn. The carved handle
is covered with coloured leather, painted in places with gold.

Documentation: Album "Ostankino." Catalogue of the exhibition of 1985, #38.

3. Lady with a Fan, 1638-1639.
Oil on canvas. 94.6 x 69.8 cm.
Wallace Collection, London.

For a long time the fan retained the role of 'wind-maker'. Even the great designer Karl Lagerfeld, in his writings about this beautiful object, dedicates his work to Aeolius, the Greek god of the winds. Although it long gave up its role as an item of any practical use, the image of the fan has always been associated with pleasant notions such as relaxation, rest, languor and even bodily or spiritual abandonment. So this elegant object became the reflection or expression of a certain kind of sensuality, a feeling of attraction for others, and a voluptuous way of life.

Painted fans originated in Japan and China. They arrived in Europe via Portugal and Spain in the 16th century. The fashion of the next few centuries, very soon made it an indispensable element of feminine dress. In 1770 there were more than 150 craftsmen making fans in Paris. Painters painted innumerable portraits of women who were almost always depicted carrying this elegant accessory...

6

4. Two-sided fan with three painted cartels. Frame with 23 openwork bone blades. Russia, around 1750. Paper, bone, taffeta, paint, sculpture, weaving, gilding. 38 x 65 cm. Gift of F. E. Vichnevski in 1958. 9207/Pz-180

The three cartels on one side of the paper sheet carry painted the personification of the three elements: Air, Earth and Water. In the left cartel, an allegory of Air is found: the skies symbolize all that is heavenly, divine, which is confirmed in the allegorical figures of Minerva, Juno and Zephyrus, situated on clouds. In the central cartel, an allegory of Earth is represented, in its daily life as it were (a scene of daily life: some children collecting the fruit of an apple tree). In the right cartel, an allegory of Water is found. On an immense stretch of sea, symbolizing the infinity of thought, small figures of two dreamers on the shore are painted. On the other side of the sheet we see a pastoral scene near an obelisk. The blades carry a chiseled design in rocaille set on a background of blue taffeta.

Documentation: Catalogue of the exhibition of 1956, #1. Album "Ostankino." Catalogue of the Exhibition of 1985, #1.

5. Two-sided fan sheet: "Games in the Park". France, middle of the 18th century.
Paper, painting. 15 x 56 cm.
Gift of F. E. Vichnevski in 1958. 9255/Pz-228
In a park, in the greenery, a group composed of young girls is represented and two young boys playing, with a knight in the centre. To the left on a bench is written in a difficult to decipher script: Crevoisy (?). On the back we see three Cupids on clouds. Documentation: Catalogue of the exhibition of 1956, #49. Catalogue of the exhibition of 1985, #8.

6. Fan: "Abigail Facing David". Frame with 20 mother-of-pearl blades.
France, around 1759. Parchment, mother-of-pearl, gold and silver sheet, painting, sculpting, inlaying. 29 x 54.3 cm.
Gift of F. E. Vichnevski in 1958.
9216/Pz-189
The parchment sheet reproduces a scene of biblical legends. Abigail is the wife of Nabal, the rich tribal chief. To avoid that her husband, who had refused his aid to David, sees all his goods pillaged, she comes on her knees to offer some bread, wine and other presents to the future king and his soldiers. On the other side, the stamp of the customs port of St Petersburg is affixed with the date: 1759. The blades carry the indented figures of ladies and cherubs and the panaches of helmeted soldiers.
Documentation: Catalogue of the exhibition of 1956, #10.

The 'wind-maker' had become an object of beauty, used in the service of flirtation, bringing great pleasure to male lovers, since women knew how to use the fan to convey far more than its original function as creator of cool breezes could have suggested. In skilful hands, the fan became a messenger of love, to the great detriment of duennas, tutors, cuckolded husbands and other jilted lovers, whom a simple movement of this small object could plunge into despair...

9

7. Two-sided fan: "The Wash of Diana". Frame with 21 mother-of-pearl blades.
Germany, around 1760.
Paper, mother-of-pearl, painting, sculpture, inlaying.
28.5 x 51 cm.
Acquired in 1985 by M. T. Audrossov.
11470/Pz-365

One side of the sheet represents, on the background of a landscape, Diana seated
among her servants. The other side represents a young girl with Cupid. In the
central part of the blades are indented representations in relief of a young girl,
a young man, and a flying Cupid.

An Ancient Marvel

The fan originated from
a double necessity: the need
to create an artificial breeze
and the necessity of protecting oneself
against insects. However, its image soon
came to include notions of comfort, pleasure and a certain degree of detachment.
In its first incarnation its appearance was
inspired by the observation of nature, in
particular the huge, broad leaves of the
palm tree. Although the principle of the
fan is very simple, and despite the fact
that until the 16th century it was
known as a 'fly-chaser', it was soon
ennobled through its use by some of
the most important people in the
world. Pharaohs in Egypt made
it a symbol of happiness and
celestial calm. It was only al-
lowed to be used by people who
were considered worthy of it. Thus it
came to feature in frescoes or on papyruses
featuring processions, festivities or even trium-
phal marches…

9. Two-sided fan representing allegorical scenes. Frame with 22 mother-of-pearl and bone blades. Germany, 1760's.
Paper, bone, mother-of-pearl, painting, sculpture.
27x42.5 cm.
Gift of E E. Vichnevski in 1958. 9239/Pz-212

One side of the sheet represents, in the centre, a couple of lovers with Cupid. To the left, on a brown chariot, we see three cherubs, one of which is crowned with laurels. Behind them, in the distance, we can see a solitary boat with a passenger. To the right of the lovers is a Cupid-Cherub with a toy: a sheep on wheels, with which a servant holding a basket of flowers plays. A small purse hangs from the servants belt. A little further to the right, a young couple walks, joined by a garland of flowers, and a seated lady plays the lyre. In the distance, Chronos watches from behind a rock as he contemplates all that is happening. The other side, the sheet represents a young couple seated in a park. The openwork bone blades, on which the figures of a lady at her table and four cherubs are represented, are placed on a mother-of-pearl base. On the mother-of-pearl panaches are indented figures of ladies.

8. Two-sided fan: "The Birth of Venus". Frame with 15 shell blades.
   France, around 1760. Paper, shell, painting, sculpting, engraving,
   gold sheet inlaying. 28.5 x 54 cm.
   Gift of F. E. Vichnevski in 1958. 9215/Pz-188

In the centre of the sheet some Tritons are represented
holding a shell, in which Venus is found. Some Cupids fly
above them. To the left, some nymphs and Tritons sail
on dolphins. To the right, a water genie watches from
behind a rock, below which swims a siren. On the other
side, we see a rocky island in a watery element
without limit with a sail in the distance. In the
upper right the stamp of the customs port of St
Petersburg is affixed. In the openwork ovals of the
frame, the same as in the mesh blades and in the
form of a column, are indented some figures of
ladies, knights, cherubs as well as some birds and
flowers.

Documentation: Catalogue of the exhibition of 1956,
#9. Catalogue of the exhibition of 1985, #4.

10. Two-sided fan representing allegorical scenes.
Frame with 22 mother-of-pearl and bone blades.
Germany, 1760's. Paper, bone, mother-of-pearl, painting,
sculpture. 27x42.5 cm.
Gift of E E. Vichnevski in 1958. 9239/Pz-212

One side of the sheet represents, in the centre, a couple of lovers with Cupid. To the left, on a
brown chariot, we see three cherubs, one of which is crowned with laurels. Behind them, in
the distance, we can see a solitary boat with a passenger. To the right of the lovers is a
Cupid-Cherub with a toy: a sheep on wheels, with which a servant holding a basket of
flowers plays. A small purse hangs from the servant's belt. A little further to the right, a
young couple walks, joined by a garland of flowers, and a seated lady plays the lyre. In the
distance, Chronos watches from behind a rock as he contemplates all that is happening. The
other side, the sheet represents a young couple seated in a park. The openwork bone blades,
on which the figures of a lady at her table and four cherubs are represented, are placed on a
mother-of-pearl base. On the mother-of-pearl panaches are indented figures of ladies.

11

First ancient Greece, then Rome turned it into an artistic object. The flabellum, as it was known in Latin, was a popular item. Beautiful Roman women used it and it became an indispensable part of their wardrobe. This enthusiasm led artists to increase the number of motifs represented on the fans and to work with more attractive or fashionable materials. The most precious example from this period comes from the Greek island of Samos and is made out of parrot feathers.

The decline of the Roman Empire and the beginning of the Middle Ages did not lead to the disappearance of the fan. Christianity, in its increasing influence worldwide, incorporated it as part of its liturgy. Its profane vocation was transformed and it was given a new symbolic role to play. Its form was adapted and its name changed. The 'wind-maker' had become a 'ripostes'.

This sacred vocation did not, however, prevent the gradual disappearance of the fan from use over the next few centuries. Perhaps in the end it was a religious interdiction which put pay to this object whose attributes had long been associated so strongly with coquetry.

11. Fan: "Gallant Scenes".
Frame with 16 bone blades.
Germany, 1770-1780.
Silk, bone, sequins, metallic thread,
painting, sculpture, embroidery, inlaying.
27.5 x 50 cm.
Gift of E. E. Vichnevski in 1958.
9244/Pz-217

In the centre of the silk sheet, surrounded
by drawings of flowers, a knight holding
a cane and a lady playing the lute are
represented. On the other side the stamp of the customs port of St. Petersburg is affixed.

Documentation: Catalogue of the exhibition of 1956, #38.
Catalogue of the exhibition of 1985, #21.

12. Fan: "The Rendez-vous".
Frame with 15 mother-of-pearl blades.
Germany, 1770-1780. Paper, silk,
mother-of-pearl, sequins, metallic thread,
painting, sculpture, embroidery,
engraving, gilding.
27 x 51.5 cm.
Gift of E. E. Vichnevski in 1958.
9242/Pz-215

In the centre of the silk sheet a scene of a
declaration of love is represented which
takes place under an arch near an altar. Cupid is holding a torch above the lovers. To the left
a washstand with a parrot, a chair and a small bench are drawn, and to the right, a harp, a
lute, a trunk and a stool. The blades represent ladies and cherubs.

Documentation: Catalogue of the exhibition of 1956, #56.

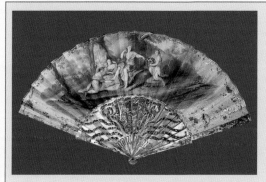

13. Two-sided fan: "The Wash of Diana".
Frame with 21 mother-of-pearl blades.
Germany, around 1760. Paper, mother-of-
pearl, painting, sculpture, inlaying.
28.5 x 51 cm.
Acquired in 1985 by M. T. Audrossov.
11470/Pz-365 One side of the sheet represents, on the background of a landscape,
Diana seated among her servants. The
other side represents a young girl with
Cupid. In the central part of the blades are
indented representations in relief of a
young girl, a young man, and a flying
Cupid.

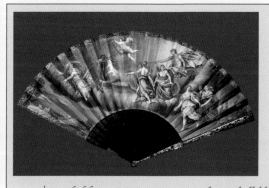

14. Two-sided fan: "Dawn". Frame with 20 shell blades.
Italy, 1760-1770.
Skin, mother-of-pearl, shell, bone, bronze, painting, sculpture, inlaying, gilding.
28.5 x 51 cm. Acquired in 1975.
1004/Pz-270

One side of the skin sheet represents a famous fresco by Guido Reni, taken from the palazzo of
Cardinal Scipion Borghese (today the Palazzo Pallavincini Rospigliosi). But the composition
is presented "as a reflection in a mirror" (reversed from right to left). Ordered by Aurora,
surrounded by female figures, symbolizing a clock, a solar chariot in which is found Apollo
moving through the sky. On the other side a marine port with a lighthouse, a fortress and a
boat is drawn. The panaches are inlaid in gilded bronze with figures of Cupids and bac-
chantes at the foot of a vine.

Documentation: Catalogue of the exhibition of 1985, #11.

15. Two-sided fan: "The Altar of Love".
Frame with 15 mother-of-pearl blades.
France, 1770-1780.
Silk, mother-of-pearl, sequins, gold and silver leaf, painting, sculpting, embroidery,
inlaying. 28 x 52 cm.
Gift of F. E. Vichnevski in 1958. 9219/Pz-192

On one side, framed with gold and silver sequins, is found, in the central cartel: a
knight, and four ladies walking in a park, as well as Cupid near the altar and two
peasants. The left cartel represents a seated lady, the right cartel: a knight leaning
against a branch. On the other side, some small bouquets are drawn in three cartels
and the stamps of the customs port of St. Petersburg is affixed. On the panaches
figures of knights are engraved.

Documentation: Catalogue of the exhibition of 1956, #13.
Documentation: Catalogue of the exhibition of 1985, #14.

In the Far East, however, the fan never ceased to be used. Its life continued, its beauty embellished by the brushes of some of China and Japan's greatest artists. In China as well as in Japan, the painted fan had existed since the second millennium BC. This version, known as a 'screen', was in the form of a picture stretched over a handle that was often made of ivory. Painters in the courts of Asia vied with each other to create the most beautiful decorations for these 'wind-makers'. Then, in the 10th century BC, the folding fan appeared in Japan. This was a much more practical object because it was less cumbersome, but above all it was more elegant because of its resemblance to a peacock's tail. Its importance as an element of female dress has not diminished since. Designed to match kimonos, used as an object for dancing, the fan became the rapier of the world of seduction...

In Europe, it was not until the Renaissance and the discoveries of the great explorers that the 'wind-maker' gradually found its true place in the world of fashion, for both men and women...

16. Fan with three painted cartels. Frame with 16 shell blades. France, 1770-1780.
Silk, shell, bone, sequins, painting, sculpting, embroidery.
27.5 x 49 cm.
Acquired in 1985 by K. V. Kouvyrdine.
11445/Pz-361

The central cartel represents a group of five people in front of the altar with Cupid. The side cartels show landscapes with flying balloons.

17. Two-sided fan painted in the "chinoiserie" style. Frame with 14 mixed blades. Holland, around 1780. Paper, bone, wood, shell, mother-of-pearl, mica, lacquer, metal leaf, fabric, painting, sculpture, inlaying, appliqué.
29.5 x 53.5 cm. Acquired in 1968 by M. I. Kalinina.
9455/Pz-253

On the paper sheet is the following image, at the same time painted and applied: a large bouquet, on the background of which two landscapes with pagodas placed in frames are presented. To the left and to the right are small scenes of Chinese genre interiors. The blades are constituted of mother-of-pearl, shell and bone. On the other side objects of daily Chinese life are drawn.

The Golden Age

The return to favour of the
fan coincided with the arrival
in Europe of the folding version,
imported from China and Japan by
Portugal and Spain, then at the height of
their powers, from the end of the 15th
century onwards. This new 'wind-maker'
gradually came into use in most European
courts. Its return to fashion coincided with a
general change in trends, with women start-
ing to wear huge, broad skirts with paniers
and padded bustles. They soon adopted this
object as a vital part of their costume and fre-
quently posed with it for the great portrait
painters of the day.

18. *Marchioness de la Solana,*
1794-95.
Canvas. 183 x 124 cm.
Louvre, Paris

19. Two-sided fan with three cartels. Frame with 17 mother-of-pearl blades. Germany, around 1780. Paper, mother-of-pearl, silver leaf, painting, inlaying, gilding. 23.5 x 48 cm.
Acquired in 1979 by N. V. Chiriaeva.
10913/Pz-299

The central cartel, on one side of the sheet, represents a group composed of three ladies, a knight and a small boy carrying a cage with a bird. The left cartel shows a lady with a stick; the right, a seated knight with two dogs. On the other side a landscape with two figures is drawn. The panaches are indented with masculine figures.

Documentation: Catalogue of the exhibition of 1980, #62. Catalogue of the exhibition of 1985, #24.

20. Fan representing a gallant scene. Frame with 14 bone blades. Germany (?), around 1780. Silk, bone, paper, metal, glass, metallic thread and sequins, painting, sculpture, embroidery, engraving. 28 x 80 cm. Acquired in 1982 by I. G. Smirnova.
11210/Pz-334

The centre of the sheet represents a seated couple, with a knight and a lady on the sides. The lady holds a fan in her hand.
Documentation: Catalogue of the exhibition of 1985, #25.

In France, it was Catherine de' Medici who was responsible for the introduction of the fan in court circles. Her favourite son, the Duc d'Anjou, became enamoured of the 'wind-maker'. In fact, the future Henri III was so crazy about the object that he was mocked for it by courtiers who were already inclined to mock him for his mannered affectations.

21. Fan sheet representing a landscape with a waterfall.
Italy, 1780-1790.
Paper, cardboard, painting. 15x43.5 cm.
Acquired in 1968 by M. I. Kalinina.
9457/Pz-256

In the central cartel a landscape with a large waterfall and two figures in the foreground is represented. In the cartels to the left and right, are motifs of the ancient world.
Documentation: Catalogue of the exhibition of 1985, #36.

22. Fan representing an urban landscape with a river. Frame with 14 bone blades.
Germany, around 1790. Silk, bone silver leaf, sequins, painting, sculpture,
embroidery, inlaying.
24.5 x 44.5 cm.
Gift of F. E. Vichnevski in 1958. 9251/Pz-224

On the silk sheet, an engraving representing a city near a river, on which a small boat is sailing with a fisherman.

Documentation: Catalogue of the exhibition of 1956, #45.
Catalogue of the exhibition of 1985, #26.

29

23. Fan with three cartels: "Werther". Frame with 15 bone blades.
England, around 1790. Silk, bone, paper, sequins, engraving, sculpture, embroidery, gilding.
28 x 52.5 cm.
Gift of F. E. Vichnevski in 1958. 9227/Pz-200

Engravings are glued on the sheet and framed with sequins. In the centre, one sees a scene
inspired by the novel by J. W. Gœthe, "The Sufferings of Young Werther". A young man is
seated at a table and he is writing a letter. To the side of him is a young woman in an
attitude of despair and a small boy carrying a pistol. The side cartels show painted
representations on the theme of antique reliefs. On the other side the stamp of the customs
port of St Petersburg is affixed with the date: 1791.

Documentation: Catalogue of the exhibition of 1956, #21.

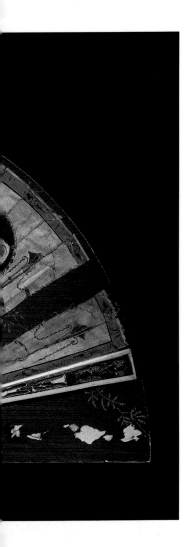

During the 17th century, the folding fan continued to grow in popularity until it became the most widely-used model. The simple screen version was still popular, even though it was on the decline. The principal centres for the manufacture of fans at the time were England, where numerous cheap models could be purchased, and Italy, where fan-makers excelled at creating very expensive painted versions. In France, the growing demand for fans at the end of the century even led to the creation of a special guild of master fan-makers.

24. Fan sheet: "The Ruins of the Antique Temple."
Italy, end of the 18th century.
Painting on skin.
17.5 x 35.5 cm.
Acquired in 1986 by L. G. Goubarvea.
11561/Pz-398

Following page :
25. Fan with five painted cartels and 15 painted bone blades.
Russia, St. Petersburg (?), around 1830.
Silk, bone, gold sequins, openwork blades in steel, painting, sculpture, embroidery.
21.7 x 41 cm.
Acquired in 1982 by G. N. Vsesviatskaïa.
11247/Pz-337

The central cartel of the silk sheet represents a couple of lovers on a background of a landscape with a church. In the side cartels, seated figures are placed; in the left, a woman; on the right, a man. The half cartels, at the extremities, present flowers. Along with sequins, the sheet is decorated with openwork and fashioned blades in oxidized steel. On the panaches a trio of musicians is painted.

Documentation: Catalogue of the exhibition of 1985, #39.

During the 18th century, France became the principal manufacturer of fans. The Age of Enlightenment was also the golden age of fans. The strictness which characterized the end of the reign of Louis XIV soon gave way to an increase in the liberty of people's behaviour. The Regency of Philippe d'Orléans, followed by the reign of Louis XV, saw this liberty develop into a kind of very refined debauchery.

The aristocracy of the time was passionate about fashion. This was the era of the fêtes galantes. The so-called petit marquis shone brilliantly in the salons while women such as the Marquise de Pompadour named marshals and controlled the destiny of the kingdom. Society lived according to the rhythm of the pamphlets of philosophers, the swish of petticoats and the tyranny of fans. So much so that some people even declared that 'The Fan of a beautiful woman is the sceptre of the world.' An Englishman even wrote that 'the Fan is so popular that a woman without a fan feels like a knight without a sword.'

26. Fan with 22 bone blades executed in the gothic style and decorated with painted embroidery: flowers, geometric figures.
Western Europe, around 1820. Bone, silk, sculpture, painting. 17.8 x 35 cm.
Acquired in 1987 by A. A. Grodski. One of the panaches carries an inscription in ink which should not be taken for the date of the creation of the fan: I. 1780.
11698/Pz-430

37

27. Two-sided fan:
"Gallant Scene in the Park". Frame with 18 chiseled
shell blades.
Germany, around 1840. Paper, mother-of-pearl, metal, gold and silver leaf,
painting, sculpture, inlaying. 28 x 51 cm.
Arrived in 1981 from the Museum of Porcelain in the Kouskovo Château of the 18th
century. Coming from the collection of L. J. Rouzskaïa.
11006/Pz-315

One side of the sheet represents a gallant group composed of seven people in a park. The
other side, in a medallion, a still-life and two pigeons are presented. On the blades
representations of swans, architectural edifices, and landscape motifs are indented.

Documentation: Catalogue of the exhibition of 1985, #59.

It gradually became a custom in
the French court for future husbands to
offer a fan to their fiancées. In Paris in the
1770s there were more than 150 workshops with
more than 6,000 people working in them from
which the future husband could choose some-
thing ravishing for his beloved.

Neither did this madness leave contemporary
writers untouched. Someone even composed an
acrostic in homage to the 'wind-maker'.

The Russian writer Derzhanin even identified
himself with the object when he wrote: 'If I
owned the whole earth, I would be a fan. My
breeze would refresh the world and I would be
a shield for the universe.'

28. Two-sided fan: "Gallant Scene in the Park". Frame with 18 chiseled shell blades. Germany, around 1840. Paper, mother-of-pearl, metal, gold and silver leaf, painting, sculpture, inlaying. 28 x 51 cm.
Arrived in 1981 from the Museum of Porcelain in the Kouskovo Château of the 18th century. Coming from the collection of L. J. Rouzskaïa.
11006/Pz-315

One side of the sheet represents a gallant group composed of seven people in a park. The other side, in a medallion, a still-life and two pigeons are presented. On the blades representations of swans, architectural edifices, and landscape motifs are indented.

Documentation: Catalogue of the exhibition of 1985, #59.

29. Two-sided fan: "The Young Sirens."
Frame with 16 mother-of-pearl blades.
France, middle of the 19th century.
Paper, mother-of-pearl, gold leaf,
painting, sculpture, inlaying,
gilding. 27.5 x 52 cm.
Gift of F. E. Vichnevski in
1958. 9223/Pz-196

In the centre, on one side of
the sheet, five young girls in
antique costume are represented on the bank of a
river, in the shade of trees.
In the side medallions, to the
left and right, couples of lovers are drawn. On the
other side, we see a pastoral scene: two male and two female
shepherds, to the side of which is a sleeping dog. A little further away are sheeps.
On the blades, inlaid with gold leaf, are representations of two ladies, a knight and motifs
of vegetation.

Documentation: Catalogue of the exhibition of 1956, #17.

30. Marriage fan with two sides. Frame with 14 chiseled mother-of-pearl blades.
Italy, 1850-1860.
Paper, mother-of-pearl, painting, sculpture, engraving, gilding. 27.5 x 51 cm.
Acquired in 1979 by P. R. Titova.
10908/Pz-298

One side of the sheet represents a scene in antique style of the dressing of a bride. At the
centre, we see the bride, behind which is a servant who holds a necklace. In front of the
bride, the groom is kneeling, represented by Hymen. To the right Cupid is presented carrying a crown and a servant bringing on a toiletry case. To the left, near a
seated woman, three Cupids braid garlands. On the other side a fashionable society is
represented in a park with a fountain. Three ladies in front of a mirror and a knight,
a servant and a page offering fruit.

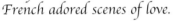

The object became exalted by people's imaginations. The 'wind-
maker' even became a means of
predicting the future. Women
amused themselves by inter-
preting the decorative motifs
on their fans, reflecting the
strong penchant for symbols
and allegories which was so
fashionable in the 18th century. Germany was passionate
about scenes symbolizing nature, abundance and the
fertility of the earth. Italy liked to feature frescoes from
Pompeii. The Dutch were keen on 'Chinoiseries', while the
French adored scenes of love.

31. Two sided fan with a painting in ink.
Frame with 16 wood blades.
   Russia, 1850-1860. Wood, leather,
      mother-of-pearl, silk, sculpture,
         weaving, ink painting.
            24 x 42.5 cm.
            Acquired in 1986 by N. V
            Diligenskaïa.
            11566/Pz-403

   Drawn on one of the sides of the thick
wood blades are, in the centre, the letter S
carrying above it a princely crown; at the
upper ends of the blades, we see the contour
of a man and woman's head, portraits in
their genre, and below them, some inscriptions in French, the contents of which vary
(memories, puns, praises to the owner of
the fan, etc.). On the other side of the sheet,
in the centre, grotesque human figures
placed horizontally, form the name:
Séraphine. On the upper part of the blades,
heads resembling portraits are also drawn,
with inscriptions (autographs) below them
and a French maxim. The autographs
belong to Nekhlioudov, Le Delobel, Basilévitch, Jazikovaïa, the Baron Guerik and others.
The panaches are covered with black leather. According to the owner, the fan belonged to
his great-grand mother Séraphine Vladimirovna Volkonskaïa.

32. Olthapage, 1877,
watercolour and pastel. 74 x 53 cm.
Brussells, Royal Museum of Fine Arts, Belgium.

33. Two-sided fan: "The Victory of Amphitrite".
Frame with 13 chiseled, gilded mother-of-pearl blades. Accompanied by a case covered with velvet.
France, around 1860. Paper, mother-of-pearl, sculpture, lithograph, typographical printing, glass, opal, gilding. 28 x 53 cm.
Acquired in 1984 in the antique shop at Moskomissiontorg, #15. 11407/Pz-355

One side of the sheet represents, in three cartels, lithographic images. The central cartel presents Amphitrite, sailing in a boat pulled by swans and framed with Cupids, elves, sirens, and nymphs. The right cartel shows Cupid, some elves and kissing doves. The left cartel depicts three Graces and some elves. On the other side, in five cartels are, in the two main cartels, a male and female shepherd, and in the others,
bouquets of flowers in vases. On the panaches, figures in the costume of the 17th century are indented: to one side, a woman; the other, a falconer with a bird in his hand.
In the interior of the case is glued the ticket: Antique fans. Fans for baskets. House Ernest Kees. Specialized in repair. 9 Boulevard des Capucines, Paris. Fans, jeweler, jewelry and lace. (The famous French company Ernest Kees, created in the 1860's, existed until the beginning of the 20th century. Many famous painters and fan specialists worked there (cf.: The Fan: Mirror of the Belle Époque, p.146)).

34. Two-sided fan representing a group of musicians. Frame with 18 chiseled mother-of-pearl blades. Accompanied by a cardboard case covered with satin. France, 1850-1860.
Paper, mother-of-pearl, colored lithograph, painting, sculpture.
27 x 51 cm.
Acquired in 1985 in the antique shop at Moskomissiontorg, #15.
11545/Pz-388

One side of the sheet represents a group of musicians composed of five people. On the other side, we see a group of five peasants near a river.

Biblical tableaux, literary themes, decorations in the style of paintings – the fan gave a home to all of these fantasies. During the course of the century Rococo style was gradually replaced by the Baroque. The 'wind-maker' followed fashion and became lighter, more flirtatious, still more refined. In the 1780s, the fan was, in the French court, an obligatory present from a future husband to his fiancée. The husband-to-be would then go around the 150 workshops with their almost 6,000 workers to find the fan which would delight his beloved.

This enthusiasm, this fashion and this passion can all to some extent explain how it was that a specific language of the fan came into existence. Messages were tapped out on the air in the salons of private mansions. Women flirted with danger, sending out signals to attract a lover, to tell him not to bother her, to instruct him to make a move for her... The fairer sex enjoyed these dangerous liaisons where reputations were made and unmade, where people obtained grace and fell into disgrace, all stemming from the simple fact of a heart expressing itself through the precise and uncompromising language of the fan...

35. Fan with a painted sheet. Frame with 16 bone blades.
Russia, end of the 19th century - beginning of the 20th century.
Silk, bone, sculpture, weaving. 32.5 x 61.5 cm.
Acquired in 1986 by M. V Milman.
11625/Pz-413

The silk sheet represents a rose branch, forget-me-nots, and white flowers.

Object
of
Fashion

The Age of Enlightenment ended with Europe ablaze and in the throes of the French Revolution, soon to be followed by the Napoleonic Empire. Society was swiftly and brutally transformed. The old order disappeared and left in its place a bourgeoisie in dire need of recognition and reassurance.

Fashion followed the vagaries of the times. Political ideas dictated trends in dress. The Sans-culottes were distinctly different from the dandies and the fine ladies. A certain austerity showed in their fashion, their Phrygian bonnets coming into conflict with the colourful opulence of the generously sized cocked hats...

37. Two-sided fan: "Group in a Park". Frame with 16 bone blades.
England (?), 1850-1860. Bone, paper, bronze, colour lithograph, gold stamping, gold and silver painting. 28.5 x 53 cm.
Arrived in 1981 from the Museum of Porcelain in the Kouskovo Château of the 18th century. Coming from the collection of L. I. Rouzskaïa. 11007/Pz-316

In a framing of gilded rocaille motifs is a group of nine people in a park, with a young man playing a guitar. On the back, in the centre of the sheet, in a medallion, a servant with a fly-swatter and a servant carrying a crown are represented.

36. Two-sided fan: "The Young Sirens". Frame with 16 mother-of-pearl blades. France, middle of the 19th century. Paper, mother-of-pearl, gold leaf, painting, sculpture, inlaying, gilding. 27.5 x 52 cm.
Gift of F. E. Vichnevski in 1958. 9223/Pz-196

In the centre, on one side of the sheet, five young girls in antique costume are represented on the bank of a river, in the shade of trees. In the side medallions, to the left and right, couples of lovers are drawn. On the other side, we see a pastoral scene: two male and two female shepherds, to the side of which is a sleeping dog. A little further away are sheep. On the blades, inlaid with gold leaf, are representations of two ladies, a knight and vegetation motifs.

  Documentation: Catalogue of the exhibition of 1956, #17.

Like most European courts, the Consulate, then the Empire, gradually moved towards a Greco-Roman style of fashion. During the Empire, balls in Paris, Vienna or Warsaw became a whirlwind of women in high-cut, straight dresses. So-called 'leg o'mutton' or 'Mameluk' sleeves came down to the elbow, revealing the silky whiteness of the forearm. The corset was no more. Close-fitting blouses came back into favour. Brassieres supported the chest. Women wore their hair 'à la Ninon', with curled hair revealing the forehead. Make-up was thick, cheeks were covered in rouge...

38. Two-sided fan: "The Bullfight".
Frame with 14 chiseled bone blades. Accompanied by a red wood case. Spain, middle of the 19th century.
Silk, bone, painting, sculpture. 28.5 x 53 cm.
Acquired in 1983 by S. P. Radimov. 11279/Pz-338

One side of the sheet represents a festival with a flamenco dance. On the other side, we see the combat of two matadors and a bull. A vine carrying grapes is represented on the chiseled and openwork blades. The central blades form a badge in relief, in which is found a basket of flowers. This fan comes from the collection of the painter P. A. Radimov.

39. Fan: "Gallant Scene with Cupids". Frame with 16 mother-of-pearl blades. Painted by Gabrielle Eylé. Accompanied by a cardboard case covered with leather. Spain, around 1870.
Skin, mother-of-pearl, painting, sculpture, gilding. 29.5 x 55.5 cm.
Acquired in 1975. 10049/Pz-272
On the left of the skin sheet a group of eight people amusing themselves is represented. A lady holds a fan while seated on the balustrade of a terrace, a couple descend some stairs leading to a body of water. Their figures coincide with the centre of the composition. A boat containing three Cupids moves towards them. To the right, near a fountain, three Cupids frolic. In the left corner is the signature: Gabrielle Eylé. The interior of the case carries a label with the inscription: A. L. "Serra". Cabaliero de Gracia. 15. #5. Carretas. Especialidad en Abanicos artísticos antiquos y modernos. (A. L. "Serra". Cabaliero de Gracia. 15. #5. Carretas. Specialized in artistic, antique and new fans).

40. Marriage fan painted on both sides. Frame with 20 openwork mother-of-pearl blades. Painted by Calamatta. From motifs of the painter Picou. Accompanied by a case in cardboard covered in satin. France, around 1870. Paper, silk, mother-of-pearl, sculpture, painting, gilding, weaving, inlaying with gold and silver leaf, braiding. 28 x 60 cm. Arrived in 1981 from the Museum of Porcelain in the 18th century Kouskovo Château. Coming from the collection of L. I. Rouszkaïa.
11004/Pz-313

One side of the sheet represents a scene of the dressing of a bride before the ceremony. On the other side, we see a chair with some small Cupids on each side, a knight and a young girl. In the side medallions Cupids praising the bride are drawn. To the right is the signature: Calamatta according to Picou. On the back of the right panache, one can read the inscription in ink: Alexandre. In the interior of the lid of the case Mag. H. Moret is inscribed in gold. According to the inscriptions, this fan was created by the Alexandre house and was sold in the store of Moret in Moscow. Josephine Calamatta (née Rochette) was born in Paris and died in 1893. Married to the famous painter and lithographer Luigi Calamatta (1802-1869), she was a portrait and genre painter. In 1875, in the sale exhibition of the Alexandre house, one of her fans was sold which carried the inscription "The Triumph of Venus" (cf.: Benezit, Vol. 2, p. 451). Henri-Pierre Picou (1824-1895), genre painter (cf.: Benezit, Vol. 8, p. 310). The two painters were specialists in the painting of fans.
Documentation: Catalogue of the exhibition of 1985, #52.

41. Mrs. Carl Meyer and her children, by J. S. Sargent.
Beginning of the 20th century.

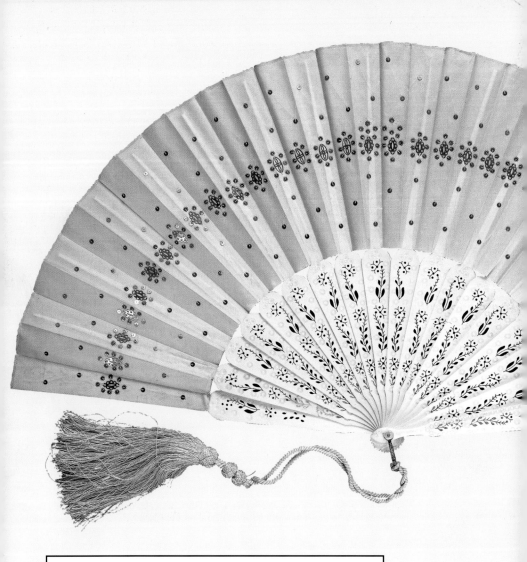

42. Fan with a silk sheet, set with sequins.
Frame with 18 bone blades.
Russia, around 1870. Silk, bone, mother-of-pearl, metallic
sequins, sculpture, embroidery, weaving, braiding.
27 x 51 cm.
Acquired in 1967 by M. A. Tchoudakova.
9378/Pz-239

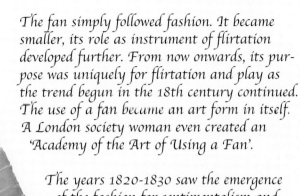

The fan simply followed fashion. It became smaller, its role as instrument of flirtation developed further. From now onwards, its purpose was uniquely for flirtation and play as the trend begun in the 18th century continued. The use of a fan became an art form in itself. A London society woman even created an 'Academy of the Art of Using a Fan'.

The years 1820-1830 saw the emergence of the fashion for sentimentalism and romanticism. Once again, ideas of feminine attraction changed. With the Romantic movement, the role of women became more reserved, more self-effacing. The gutsy and assertive female revolutionary woman had been completely supplanted.

43. Fan with plaited sheet. Fashion engraving from the journal "Modnyi svet" ("The World of Fashion"). 1877.

44. Fan with a lace sheet. Frame with 17 gilded mother-of-pearl blades.
Accompanied by a cardboard case covered in satin and lined with silk.
France, around 1880.
Lace, mother-of-pearl, metal, weaving, sculpture, gilding. 35 x 67 cm.
Acquired from the antique shop at Moskomissiontorg, #15.
11490/Pz-369

45. Fan with a sheet of painted silk. Frame with 18 mother-of-pearl blades. Painted by Dailliard. Accompanied by a cardboard case covered in satin.
France, around 1880. Silk, mother-of-pearl, bone, lace, satin, metal, sculpture, painting, weaving. 32.5x61 cm.
Arrived in 1984 with national funds of Moskomissiontorg.
11428/Pz-356

The silk sheet represents, in a framing of lace, rose bushes and lilac branches, above which are found two butterflies and a bee. To the right, we see the signature: Dailliard. On the blades motifs of flowers are indented and painted in gold and silver.
The interior of the lid of the case carries a ticket: A. Ralley and Co. Kouznetski bridge, Solodovnikov house, Moscow.

The uncompromising dictates of fashion banished all former references to ancient Greece and Rome. Waists became lower, materials were worn in thick layers. Skirts widened, the décolleté disappeared (except for evening occasions).
The corset was back in fashion, the wasp waist was de rigueur. Accessories were imbued with a romanticism that was rich in medieval symbolism. Fans opened out onto allegories featuring temples to Love and Friendship, weeping willows – a symbol of melancholy – and multitudes of flowers.

These motifs were often made of coloured silk and sequins. Many of the fans of this period were also made from bone, horn or shell. The Romantic passion for Gothic styles showed through the way they were made.

46. Fan: "The Young Girl and the Doves". Frame with 18 mother-of-pearl blades. Painted by Sarita. France, around 1880. Lace, silk, mother-of-pearl, bone, metal, sculpture, painting, weaving, braiding, inlaying with metallic leaf. 35 x 62 cm.

Arrived in 1981 from the Museum of Porcelain in the Kouskovo Château of the 18th century. Coming from the collection of L. I. Rouszkaïa.
11003/Pz-312
The silk insertion at the centre of the lace sheet represents a seated young girl holding a cage in her hand. To the side of her swirl two doves and Cupid. Below is the signature: Sarita. The mother-of-pearl blades are inlaid garlands of gold and silver leaf.

Documentation: Catalogue of the exhibition of 1985, #58.

47. Satin fan representing a bouquet.
Frame with 18 bone blades.
Russia, around 1880.
Satin, bone, wood, metal, silk thread, painting, sculpture,
milling, twisting. 35 x 66.5 cm.
Acquired in 1980 by N. G. Maximova.
10983/Pz-310

Documentation: Catalogue of the
exhibition of 1985, #73.

49. Fashion engraving from the journal,
"Der Bazar, illustrierte Damen-
Zeitung". 1892.

48. Satin fan painted with flowers and
carrying the inscription: "souvenir".
Frame with 18 bone blades.
Russia, 1880-1890. Satin, bone, metal, painting, sculpture.
32 x 61 cm. Acquired in 1979 by E. M. Koudrina-
Borissoglebskaïa.
10918/Pz-304

Documentation: Catalogue of the exhibition of 1985, #50.

By the middle of the
19th century, the charms of
the Age of the Enlightenment were
being rediscovered. Castles, knights
and troubadours continued to be depicted on fans, but
in a new way. 'Historicism' became the dominant style.
Across Europe, fan-makers also rediscovered the
charms of mythological scenes and literary themes.

50. Fan with a painted black sheet. Frame with 18 pierced wood blades.
France, beginning of the 20th century. Silk, wood, sequins, metal,
painting, sculpture, embroidery, weaving, inlaying. 35 x 66 cm.
Acquired in 1985 by V. N. Naourits.
11508/P7-382
The black silk sheet represents, in the painting and with the
sequins, a cornucopia, flowers and butterflies. Under the design
is the signature: G. Tutin. The interior of the lid of the case
carries the inscription: Faucon. Maker of fans. Repairs.
38, Avenue de l'Opéra. Ancient passage of the Panoramas. (The
fan maker E. Faucon functioned until the 1880's. In the 1890's,
the owner of the factory merged his company with that of E. Kees.
(cf.: The Fan: Mirror of the Belle Epoque, p. 148)).

Nevertheless, there are some motifs on fans which
never changed: idyllic pastoral scenes and scenes of
love have been a staple of fan decoration for
centuries.
During the Industrial Revolution, this object of
flirtation become available to the less well-off
strata of society. The bourgeoisie, like some of the
clergy, used them. And for this new clientele, the
fan-makers proposed a new style of decoration, creating
models decorated with scenes from everyday life and
historical events depicted in a very realistic style.

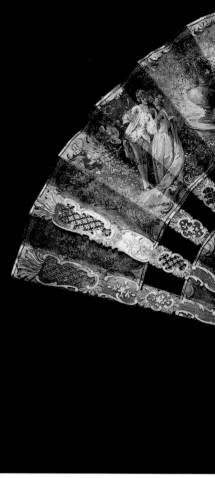

52. Grand Duchess Elisabeth Fedorovna.

53. Fan with two band sheets: "Gallant
Scenes in the Park". Frame with 18
chiseled cellulose blades. Painted by Jules
Donzel. Accompanied by a cardboard
case. France, around 1890. Paper, silk,
cellulose, metal, paste, painting, sculpture,
weaving. 26.7 x 51 cm.
Acquired in 1986 by V. I. Zametseva.
11564/Pz-401

The sheet of the fan is comprised of two distinctly painted paper bands, held together by the blades. On the upper band, we see three scenes. A little to the left of the centre is a knight welcoming a woman, carrying a chair. To the left are a couple of lovers in a park. To the right, a knight on a balcony tosses flowers to a lady holding an umbrella.

On the lower sheet, narrower, is drawn a marine landscape with boats and a waterfall to the right. To the left, in the upper band, is the signature: J. Donzel, son. On the back of the right panache, E. Kees is inscribed in gold. The interior of the lid of the case carries the inscription in stamped gold: E. Kees. Maker of Fans. 8 Boulevard des Capucines. Paris.

New materials were also used. After 1850, fans made from lace, satin, velvet and ostrich feathers became very popular. This period coincides with the arrival of the department store in France. From Bon Marché to Printemps, via le Bonheur des Dames, as immortalized by Emile Zola, this massive change led to the 'democratisation' of fashion accessories like the fan. At the same time, the confirmation of Charles Frederick Worth in the 1860s as the undisputed leader of European fashion meant that Paris became the capital of fashion. This was the Second Empire - the period of crinolines and whalebone corsets. For evenings, white gloves were worn with a white fan, which would often have been made of mother-of-pearl.

1870-1871 saw German unity impose itself on the ashes of a French empire which had been defeated on the battlefield. France became a republic and fashions changed yet again. Gone were crinolines, in their place was a style known as 'tapestry'. The important players here were the hard-working bourgeoisie, eager to refine themselves and flaunt their wealth. Dresses were made like curtains, covered in ribbons, frills and furbelows. The corset became very tight, creating a powerful effect of curvaceousness. The bustle was supposed to point in one direction and the chest in the other. Designers such as Doucet, Redfern, and then Maggy Rouff become leaders of fashion.

55. Fan with 20 openwork bone blades.
Russia, end of the 19th century.
Bone, silk, mother-of-pearl, sculpture, weaving. 27 x 35 cm.
Acquired in 1967 by M. A. Tchoudakova.
9379/Pz-240
Documentation: Catalogue of the exhibition of 1985, #47.

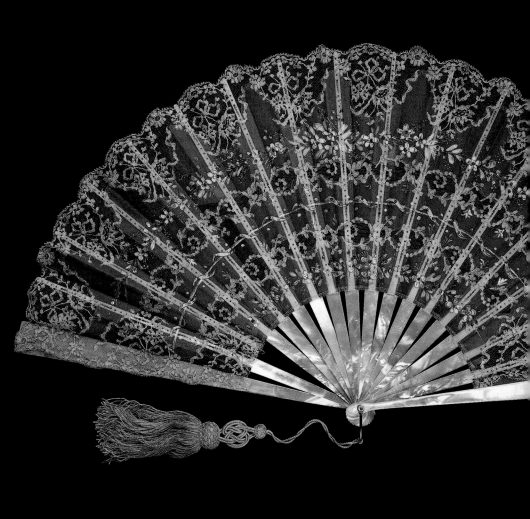

56. Fan with a sheet of silk and lace. Frame with 18 mother-of-pearl blades,
accompanied by a case.
Russia, end of the 19th century.
Silk, mother-of-pearl, lace, sequins, sculpture, painting, embroidery, braiding, weaving.
29.5 x 54.5 cm.
Acquired in 1986 by N. A. Pletneva.
11673/Pz-432
On the silk sheet garlands of flowers interlaced with a ribbon are placed.

57. Countess de Benavente, 1785.
Oil on canvas. 104 x 80 cm.
Bartolomé March Severa, Madrid.

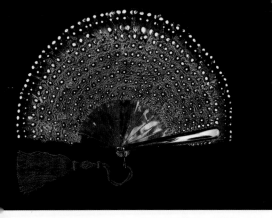

59. Fan with a sheet of black watered fabric.
Frame with 14 wood blades, openwork and pierce
Russia, end of the 19th century.
Wood, metal, sculpture, weaving. 27.5 x 52 cm.
Acquired in 1986 by N. P. Pigareva.
1168/Pz-435

This fan belonged to the granddaughter of the p
F. I. Tioutchev, E. I. Pigareva (née Tioutchev).

58. Fan fashioned in pheasant feathers. Frame
with 16 shell blades.
Russia, end of the 19th century. Shell, feathers,
sculpture, arrangement. 24 x 37 cm.
Acquired in 1985 by L. G. Savtchenko.
11518/Pz-418

However, the ravages of time still did not prevent the fan from remaining an essential part of the female wardrobe. Throughout the century, it managed to retain its importance. Its form and image changed as fashions changed, but its durability was due to what women had made of it: a vital element of seduction. The fan had, since the Age of Enlightenment, become an accomplice in women's 'affairs'. The language which grew from its use continued to be perfected during a period of increasing puritanism, only making the lovers' game more refined and more thrilling. Duennas and tutors had to be ever more vigilant of their charges.

As the end of the 19th century approached, the fan continued to change along with women's fashions, basking in its role as the armed hand of women's hearts and changing its image like a chameleon. The end of the century brought a complete revolution in architectural style with the arrival of the Art Nouveau movement. Women's figures adapted and changed once again, this time rejecting straight lines in favour of the S-shaped curves favoured by the age. A new type of corset followed. Decorative motifs were essentially floral, in the style of the Parisian metro entrances designed by Guimart. Trees, flowers and all things connected with nature gave fashion a bright, colourful elegance. And Paris, the city of light, was the place where fashions were made and broken under the talented scissors of the Callot sisters, Jeanne Paquin, or Jeanne Lanvin.

60. Lace fan carrying the monogram A. A. Tatischeva. Frame with 18 cellulose blades. Accompanied by a cardboard case. Russia, end of the 19th century. Lace, cellulose, metal, weaving, sculpture, gilding.
27 x 53 cm.
Acquired in 1981 by A. V. Kamenskaïa.

11150/Pz-327
One of the panaches carries the monogram in gilded bronze: A. T. This fan belonged to the countess Tatischeva Alexandra Alexandrovna (née Volodimerova), wife of the member of the Ministry of the Interior,

Modes Parisiennes.

the count V.S. Tatischev (Tatischev S. S., *The Tatischevs. 1400-1900. Historical and Genealogical Study.* St. Petersburg, 1900).

Documentation: Catalogue of the exhibition of 1985, #45.

61. Fashion plate, taken from the magazine "Modes parisiennes: Bureau des modes et costumes historiques".

62. Fan with a sheet of blue feathers.
Frame with 11 blue wood blades.
Russia, end of the 19th century-beginning of the 20th century.
Wood, feathers, sculpture, engraving, painting in silver and blue
gouache. 22.5x49 cm.
Acquired in 1979 by G. M. Koudrina-Borissoglebskaïa.
10917/Pz-303

The fan was still around, this time accompanying tailored outfits worn with a very short spencer. In the evenings, the fan would complete an outfit consisting of a very low-cut, long dress, with a tailored coat with leg o'mutton sleeves worn over the top.

Just as there are great dress designers, so there are great masters of the craft of fan-making. Some Parisian workshops became famous all over the world: Derochers, Kees, or Duvelleroy seduced their customers by the sheer beauty of the fans in their catalogues. Many of the greatest fan-makers were also painters and artisans of immense talent. The most famous of all was the Maison Alexandre, at 14, Boulevard Montmartre. Here, the crowned heads of Europe came to buy their fans, with the French Empress Eugenie, Queen Victoria of England, and the Russian Empress Alexandra Fedorovna among its most faithful customers.

63. Fan with a sheet of white ostrich feathers.
Frame with 20 cellulose blades.
Russia, end of the 19th century-beginning of the 20th century. Feathers, cellulose, silk,
metal, sculpture, melting, weaving. 32 x 54 cm.
Acquired in 1985 by G. I. Baumstein. 11505/Pz-379

64. Auguste Renoir. "Girl with a fan", 1880. Oil on canvas. 65 x 50 cm. The Hermitage, St Petersburg.

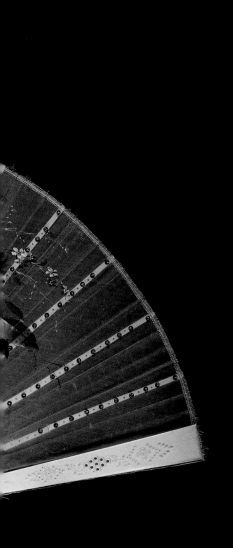

65. Fan representing a bouquet of flowers. Frame with 16 bone blades.
Russia, end of the 19th century- beginning of the 20th century. Silk, bone, grains of glass, sequins, metal leaf, painting, sculpture, embroidery, engraving, weaving, inlaying.
20.5 x 65 cm.
Acquired in 1968 by A. G. Gladkovskaïa.
9658/Pz-264

The sheet, in transparent silk, represents a bouquet composed of a green branch, roses and blue flowers. Along the panaches, the sheet has steel sequins with little grains of transparent glass on the interior.

66. Two-sided fan in the Art Nouveau style. Frame with 20 bone blades.
Painted by V. France. In between the 19th and 20th centuries.
Paper, bone, metal, painting, sculpture, melting, engraving. 27 x 50.5 cm.
Acquired in 1978 by S. M. Michtchenko.
10819/Pz-274
One side of the sheet represents five female figures in the costume of the 11th century up to
the 15th century. Under each of them is a date and an inscription. On the other side is a
large half figure of a woman in medieval costume. On each side is a coat of arms. At the
bottom, on the left, we can see the inscription: V Paris. The design of vegetation engraved
on the bone blades is covered in gold.
Documentation: Catalogue of the exhibition of 1985, #77.

In terms of its shape, the fan was getting wider. The blades were more delicate and longer, making them ever more elegant. The motifs, which decorated them, borrowed from the new trends in fashion: use of darker colours and translucent materials reflected the two popular symbols of Art Nouveau, day and night. Floral decorations added to the evanescence of the humble 'wind-maker'.

67. Fashion engraving from the journal, "The Season. Illustrated Ladies Journal", 1870.

This new beauty could scarcely leave people unmoved. Just as during the Age of Enlightenment, the fan provided ample inspiration for poets. The writer Vrangel wrote an essay on Spain entitled 'Blood and the Fan': 'The Fan, an instrument of malice and affectation, the little fan, often black as a sign of mourning, moves ceaselessly in the hands of all women, as if it were chasing the spirit of the word 'blood'. Everywhere in the streets, in the houses, in modest lodging and the luxurious apartment alike, the fan moves, like the pulse of life, throughout Spain'.

69. Fashion engraving from the journal *"Parisian Fashions: Office of Historic Fashions and Costumes"*, 1807.

68. Lace. Fan representing flying Cupids. Frame with 18 wood blades. Russia, beginning of the 20th century.
Silk, lace, wood, painting, weaving.

35,5 x 66,5 cm.
Acquired in 1973 by L. M. Kotovskaïa.
10003/Pz-269
Documentation: Catalogue of the exhibition of 1985, #68.

70. Black silk lace fan. Frame with 18 black wood blades. Russia, beginning of the 20th century. Silk, lace, wood, braiding, weaving. 35 x 66 cm. Acquired in 1979 by N. V. Chiriaeva. 10916/Pz-302
Documentation: Catalogue of the exhibition of 1985, #71.

These few lines can hardly fail to conjure up the image
of those Sevillian women who, under the blazing heat of
the Andalusian sun, would put on their most beautiful
flounced dresses and cover their shoulders with
mantillas of fine lace. Thus dressed, these proud women
would stand concealed, observing the populace moving
to and fro under the balconies whence they held sway,
proud and sublime. In their hands, the fan does not
just perform its function, it positively dances.

Alas, these times of subtle elegance are long gone. Today a fan is more likely to be associated with eccentricity or some kind of folkloric ritual. Its intimate role in women's affairs has continued to decline. Only in Asia has this beautiful accessory retained some measure of use, although it is now more commonly decorated with commercial motifs than anything artistic: most big companies in Japan offer clients 'utchiwas' decorated with corporate logos and slogans.

For the lover of beautiful fans there remains only nostalgia for an object that has been in turn made divine and sacred, hidden and revealed and that above all has been close to women's hearts. Having become so precious, today the fan can only excite a certain form of melancholy.

71. Satin fan embroidered with a representation of flowers and butterflies. Frame with 16 bone blades.
Russia, beginning of the 20th century.
Satin, lace, silk, bone, chenille, sculpture, embroidery, weaving, 32.7 x 62 cm.
Aquired in 1981 in the antique shop at Moskomissiontorg, #15. 11028/Pz-321

Documentation: Catalogue of the exhibition of 1985, #75.

72. Lady with a glove-puppet and a fan, 1873.
Handcoloured print, 32 x 22 cm.
Signed at bottom right: Félicien Rops.
Namur, provincal museum Félicien Rops.

73. Fan with a sheet of goose feathers, painted in Japanese style with flowers and birds. Frame with 28 wood blades.
Russia, beginning of the 20th century.
Wood, feathers, illumination, sculpture, gilding, 31 x 49 cm.
Acquired in 1985 by E. M. Savonina.
11474/Pz-367

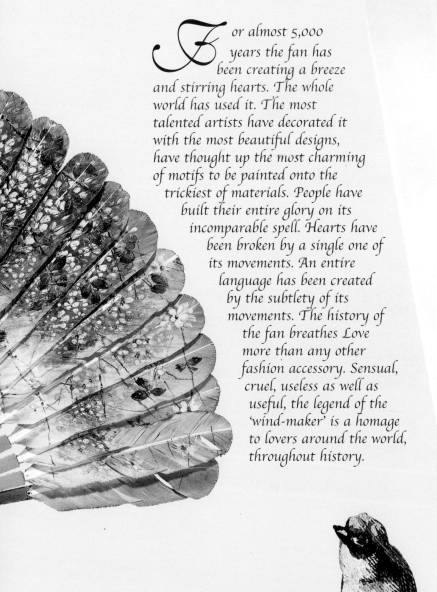

For almost 5,000 years the fan has been creating a breeze and stirring hearts. The whole world has used it. The most talented artists have decorated it with the most beautiful designs, have thought up the most charming of motifs to be painted onto the trickiest of materials. People have built their entire glory on its incomparable spell. Hearts have been broken by a single one of its movements. An entire language has been created by the subtlety of its movements. The history of the fan breathes Love more than any other fashion accessory. Sensual, cruel, useless as well as useful, the legend of the 'wind-maker' is a homage to lovers around the world, throughout history.

74. Stage fan of an actrice of the Marie Theater in St Petersburg, N.V. Petrova. Russia, around 1910. Palace of Ostankino in Moscow.

The Language of the Fan

in the 18th Century

To yawn behind one's fan: Go away, you bore me.
To lift the fan towards the right shoulder: I hate
you.
To lower the closed fan towards the floor: I scorn
you, I despise you.
To lightly touch the closed fan to one's right eye:
When shall I see you?
To signal towards oneself with the fan closed: I
always want to be with you.
To threaten with the fan closed: Do not be too
bold, audacious.
To raise the fan with the right hand: Are you
faithful to me?
To hide the eyes behind one's fan: I love you.
To offer a fan: You please me very much.
To conceal one's left ear with the closed
fan: Do not disclose our secret.
To hold the fan over one's heart: I am
yours for life.
To slowly close one's fan: I agree
completely, I accept all that you say.

V Pokrovski. "Elegance in the Satirical
Literature of the 18th Century".
Moscow, 1903, p. 43.

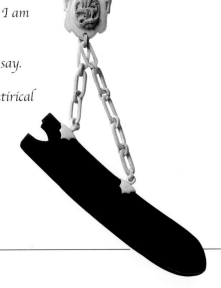

The Language of the Fan in the 19th Century

To completely open one's fan: I am thinking it over.

To place one's hand over the heart while holding the fan open in front of the eyes: I love you.

To indicate the floor near oneself with the fan: Come close to me.

To press the open fan with both hands against one's breast while slowly lifting the eyes: I humbly request forgiveness.

To lightly touch one's mouth repeatedly with the closed fan: Could I speak with you in private?

To completely open one's fan and wave it in the direction of one's interlocutor: I would hope to always be with you.

To look at one's closed fan: I think of you all the time.

To hold lightly with the left hand the closed fan over one's heart: Are you faithful to me?

The number of unopened blades indicate the time of a rendez-vous: At the agreed hour.

To turn the inside face of the fan towards one's interlocutor: I shall not be able to come.

To move the end of the fan on the palm of one's hand, as if writing a letter: I will let you know by mail.

To wave away one's interlocutor with the closed fan: I do not like you.

To direct the open fan towards the floor: I despise you.

To open and close the fan repeatedly: You are too bold, audacious.

75. Souvenir fan: "The bullfight". Spain, 1910's.
Palace of Ostankino in Moscow.

To angrily close the fan and turn it feverishly in one's hand: I am angry with you.
To press one's chin against the closed fan: I am sulking.
To write with the finger on the outside of the fan: Let me know by mail.
To look at one's open fan while rocking the head from side to side: You do not want to know me at all.
To turn with the right hand the end of the closed fan held in the left hand: You are being deceived.
To hold the two ends of the closed fan between the palms: I require an answer.
To indicate a seat with the fan closed: Sit next to me.
To indicate a seat with the fan open: That's enough! You are boring me.
To point several times to one's forehead with the fan closed: Are you mad?
To press one's chin on the open fan: Stop your repugnant pleasantries.
To press the closed fan against one's right shoulder: I detest you.
To repeatedly drop the closed fan half open into the left hand: Not another word.
To flutter the open fan towards oneself: Dance with me.
To cover the palm of the left hand with the open fan held in the right hand: Keep it secret.
To give the closed fan to one's interlocutor: You please me very much.

To place the open fan against the right cheek: Yes.
To place the open fan against the left cheek: No.
To place the closed fan against the right ear: I am listening to you.
To hold the closed fan to the right temple: Stop being jealous.
To gracefully open and close one's fan: Your desires shall be fulfilled.
To lay the closed fan in the fold of the left hand: I do not understand you.
To gracefully hold out the open fan to one's interlocutor: Welcome.
To impatiently pass the closed fan from one hand to the other: I am very worried.
While holding the open fan with the right hand to make it turn with the left hand: My parents do not wish it.
To tap with the closed fan between the fingers of the left hand: We must interrupt our conversation.
To press the closed fan to one's heart while holding it with both hands: Spare me this unbearable company.
To hang the closed fan from the right hand: Adieu, good-bye.

V. Pokrovski. "Elegance in the Satirical Literature of the 19th Century". p. 44-46.

77. Fan with a satin sheet, representing a flowering branch of a wild rose bush.
Frame with 16 pierced bone blades.
Russia, beginning of the 20th century.
Silk, bone, metal, mother-of-pearl, painting, sculpture, weaving, 28.5 x 64 cm.
Acquired in 1984 by S. N. Gousseva.
11390/Pz-349